It is in the art of the poster that artists use their imagination and invention to unashamedly celebrate and reveal the uniqueness of the New Zealand scene.

HAMISH KEITH
CULTURAL HISTORIAN

N·Z·R

SELLING THE DREAM

CLASSIC NEW ZEALAND TOURISM POSTERS

NEW ZEALAND

First published in 2016 by New Holland Publishers Pty Ltd
London • Sydney • Auckland

www.newhollandpublishers.com

5/39 Woodside Ave, Northcote, Auckland 0627, New Zealand

A catalogue record for this book is available from the
National Library of New Zealand.

ISBN 978 1 86966 444 2

Managing Director: David Cowie
Publisher: Christine Thomson
Design: Peter Alsop and The Gas Project
Production Director: Olga Dementiev
Printer: Toppan Leefung Printing Ltd

10 9 8 7 6 5 4 3 2

Keep up with New Holland Publishers on Facebook
www.facebook.com/NewHollandPublishers

CONTENTS

WINTER SPORTS AT TONGARIRO NATIONAL PARK

NEW ZEALAND

FOREWORD

Canterbury Museum is immensely proud to have developed *Selling the Dream*, the exhibition touring throughout New Zealand in 2015–17. It is also deeply satisfying that the beautiful content of the exhibition will live on through this legacy publication.

During the exhibition's opening season at Canterbury Museum, our team was thrilled by the response to these evocative works of art. Visitors from here and abroad told us that these posters generated feelings of nostalgia; revealed a world of art previously unrecognised; and were a fascinating celebration of Aotearoa New Zealand. We also heard frequently how blown away visitors were by the skills of New Zealand's early poster artists.

In *Selling the Dream*, more than 50 posters from the 1920s to the 1960s promote the glamour of travel and New Zealand's tourism attractions of the day. They are stunning and arresting works, designed to be absorbed at a glance, yet memorable enough to subsequently secure a visit to New Zealand or a domestic adventure by New Zealanders. The posters were critical to building New Zealand's tourism brand and industry. Equally importantly, they helped shape how we think of ourselves as New Zealanders.

The exhibition would not have been possible without the generous support of private collectors who loaned their posters, along with the passion of Peter Alsop. Peter approached us with a proposal to work together to ensure New Zealanders could enjoy these posters again. We are also grateful to Warren Feeney and Richard Wolfe who worked with our own curatorial team to research and develop the exhibition.

Far beyond a popular exhibition, *Selling the Dream* reminds us of the natural beauty of New Zealand and the diversity of tourism experiences within easy reach. As the Government Tourist Department once touted, New Zealand really is 'a world in itself'. We're delighted this book has been produced to celebrate New Zealand tourism and the great posters and artists that did so much to define it.

Anthony Wright
Director, Canterbury Museum

INTRODUCTION

In 1901, New Zealand took a bold step by establishing the world's first government tourist department; a landmark decision in the history of New Zealand's tourism industry and wider economic prosperity. *Selling the Dream* unveils the story of how vintage travel posters helped build the industry and a national identity along the way.

TOURISM BEGINNINGS

While the Department of Tourist and Health Resorts was central to galvanising an organised tourism effort, there were pivotal publicity events before. New Zealand's earliest promotion was publicity about Cook's voyages and, in a related but more commercial sense, the efforts from 1837 of the London-based New Zealand Company to promote emigration to New Zealand. Amongst the effort were prints – kauri trees and all – by Company draughtsman Charles Heaphy; amongst the best known of all nineteenth-century New Zealand images.

The word was out that New Zealand had plenty to offer, something Prince Alfred's visit to the Pink and White Terraces in 1870 would also broadcast to the world. Ironically, the loss of the Terraces to the Tarawera Eruption in 1886 would also build interest, including 12 years later – such was their potent mystique – when they featured on the world's first pictorial stamps. Spectacular and unpredictable geothermal activity, epitomised by the eruption, would be New Zealand's start to adventure tourism and great fodder for early tourism publicity.

With that backdrop, it's no surprise that the Department's efforts were initially focused on Rotorua, 'the metropolis of geyserland'. It was also the epicentre of Māori culture, reflected by the choice of 'Maoriland' as the Department's first cable address (think Twitter handle today). In the Department's first year, the Duke and Duchess of York would visit and be gifted a 3-metre model of the Te Arawa ancestral canoe, piled high with Māori artefacts.

Left: This small-format poster from 1904, three years after the establishment of the Tourist Department, is an example of how posters and publicity at that time typically relied on text descriptions and black-and-white illustration. The Department's 'Cable' address – MAORILAND – appears at the bottom, much like a Facebook or Twitter address today. Aimed at potential settlers, the back of this poster also promoted 'some of the chief features of State control and national enterprise in New Zealand, the outcome of a high endeavour to thoroughly develop the colony's resources and to shut out the social misery of older lands'.

Maoridom was a huge asset – New Zealand's exotica – with a public line of 'no racial problem in these happy isles'. In reality, it was a time of significant poverty for Māori and cultural appropriateness was also not part of the publicity brief. For example, images of Māori wearing ceremonial garb for daily duties were culturally wrong, and tourists discovering most Māori didn't routinely wear flax skirts or feather cloaks came as a real surprise. Even today, New Zealanders enjoy a 'tiki tour' – a wandering exploration – despite trivialisation of 'hei tiki', a significant culture artefact. Plump and comical warriors on official publicity, and straw hats on important cultural architecture, probably top the cringe.

Rotorua's pull would increase in 1908 with the completion of the Tudor-style bathhouse, the largest building of its style outside England. The Government wanted to compete with the sophistication of international spas and felt a world-famous spa-town would attract thousands more visitors each year. The Government was right but, like all good investment strategies, 'taking the waters' in Rotorua was far from the full picture. For diversification, the Department's first leader Thomas Donne, a keen outdoorsman himself, was well-attuned to the potential of the 'Sportsman's Paradise' – skiing, hunting, trout fishing, climbing and deep-sea fishing. This would quickly become an alluring tourism proposition and a very striking theme for poster artists wanting to make their mark.

A range of savvy marketing techniques were employed, and make for impressive reading in the Department's early Annual Reports, well before marketing got its name. In 1905, the Department invited Englishman Samuel Turner to climb, anticipating his articles, books and photographs would publicise New Zealand to enthusiasts abroad. Well-known American writer and big-game fisherman Zane Grey also made multiple visits and wrote articles for US magazines – a bit like today's tweets. On Grey's first trip, he remarked 'New Zealand waters are undoubtedly the most remarkable in the seven seas ... there is no doubt that the preservation of the fish and proper publicity will add immensely to New Zealand's prosperity'.

Private investors also lent a hand. Rodolph Wigley was the most well-known, pioneering package tourism by embracing different transport options and hospitality. In a wink to his European competitors, Wigley's Mount Cook Motor Company promoted a 'Grand Tour'; there was no need for Paris or London when Timaru could be connected with the Hermitage with table tennis at night. Wigley would later go on to build the Chateau Hotel at Mt Ruapehu in 1929, which became an iconic building in early tourism art. The Chateau was a sophisticated statement but soon a commercial failure with the Government taking ownership and using it for wartime convalescence.

Right: This poster published by the Railways Department, one of the earliest travel posters known to exist (1889), underscores the important role played by rail in building New Zealand's tourism industry. Typical of posters of that time, the poster is full of information and the illustrations are detailed; a marked contrast to the simplified poster style that later emerged. Source: Auckland Libraries, NZ Map 6573, 83 x 56cm.

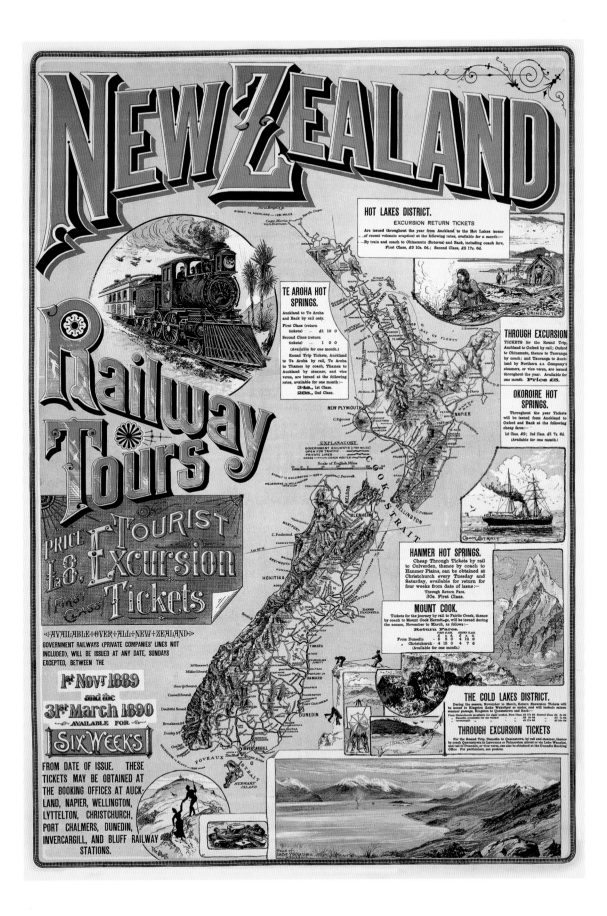

Notwithstanding ups and downs, the tourism industry flourished and went hand-in-hand with growing prosperity, in part a reflection of New Zealand becoming Britain's farm. Agriculture and tourism helped each other, reputationally and economically. Tourism publicity celebrated 'the pastoral paradise' and an image of a kiwi was used to sell lamb, while butter was promotionally barged down the River Thames. The Tourist Department would later describe refrigerated shipping as the most important event in New Zealand's first 100 years. Tourism was, and remains, inextricably linked to New Zealand's progress.

THE POWER OF THE POSTER

Besides the Tarawera Eruption, 1886 was a significant year for another reason. Britain's Great Western Railway created the first railways advertising department, sensing the growing importance of travel publicity and a radical move to pictorial posters. This evolution seems trivial now, as if advertising has always embodied art, but the innovation was significant – from dull-but-functional typeset posters to the use of illustration.

Early illustrations trumped text, but were often simplistic, flat and awkward. Illustration itself needed to evolve and find an art form that, given posters work or fail in a glance, was up to the urgent task. German Lucian Bernhard would lead it, his 1906 poster for matches simplifying the subject to essential colours and form. Called *Plakatstil* – German for 'poster style' – in 1922 it would become known as graphic design. It quickly became the heart of commercial art with widespread implications for global commerce, including a radical new standard and impact of tourism art.

Central to this evolution was Paris's 1925 International Exposition of Modern Industrial and Decorative Arts. Here, the Art Deco style emerged, named from an abbreviation of the Expo's French title. This was one of the most pivotal events in the history of poster art and very contagious in New Zealand. Leonard Mitchell's *Blue Baths* (page 116) is perhaps the most overt Art Deco design, with an elegance and simplicity that cannot have been as effortless as it looks. Around this time, the Governor General, Lord Bledisloe, also helped kick commercial art along, exhibiting his collection of posters from leading global artists.

Just as ideas travelled, it was the rise of transportation that took posters into a golden age. Railway stations were on the rise and prime real estate for advertising travel and other things. Trackside hoardings were also big business and the subject of much debate about

Right: Early on, the Railways Department leased adjoining land to its rail network to private advertisers. The establishment of a Railways Advertising Branch in 1915, followed by the Department's own design studio in 1920 ('Railways Studios'), changed the advertising game. The proliferation of advertising hoardings, and signs and posters at railway stations, helped fuel New Zealand's social and economic development. Hoarding adverts, like the Hudsons illustration on the right, were hand-painted and constituted some of New Zealand's earliest large-scale paintings. Source: *Auckland Weekly News* Christmas Number 1928.

whether they improved or scarred the landscape. Governments and railways reached agreements for showing each other's wares, and developments in printing technology nudged things further along. Tourism helped commerce and commerce helped tourism – a powerful dependency that the poster movement would both fuel and exploit.

NEW ZEALAND'S TRAVEL POSTER PROGRESS

What unfolded in New Zealand was a collection of posters that portrayed the country's best assets in an alluring and evocative way. While other countries touted resorts, hotels and sophistication, New Zealand artists celebrated raw beauty. Arresting images would bring multiple campaign messages to life, including 'Scenic Wonderland', 'Playground of the Pacific', 'Sportsman's Paradise', 'Maoriland', 'Brighter Britain of the South', 'God's Custodian' and 'A World in Itself'.

But like other endeavours, to get to simplicity, difficulty must first be traversed. It has to be recognised that, initially, there was no New Zealand brand and no clear national identity. Tourists – with Paris, Rome and London on their doorstep – also needed to be convinced that sailing 6.5 weeks by boat, each way, was worthwhile. Posters themselves were also in competition, up against the world's best designers. Like an impatient younger sibling, the youngest country in the world stepped up to this challenge and made a significant impact on the world stage.

While a range of publicity techniques were used early on, the first mention of 'poster' in the Tourist Department's Annual Report was in 1915. It was the same year the Railways Department opened its own Advertising Branch to manage trackside hoardings, followed by the establishment of its own design studio in 1920, the Railways Studios. From this time, an extensive poster and outdoor advertising drive would underpin New Zealand's development; not just in terms of tourism but wider economic and social activity as well.

Left: Cheap Travel by Train dates from about 1935 and uses the circular motion of locomotive wheels and different scenic attractions to convey the ease of travel in New Zealand. A statement about cost-effectiveness takes away any residual doubt for the potential traveller. The poster is held in Archives New Zealand (R18837562), an important collection of early tourism publicity, alongside the impressive collection of the Alexander Turnbull Library.

Following pages: The Railways Studios was established in 1920, headed by Stanley Davis, and quickly became a formidable force in outdoor advertising in New Zealand. Barry Ellis joined the Studios in 1953 as an apprentice, ultimately graduating to Head Designing Artist before his resignation in 1972. Ellis loved every minute of it; fuelling a life-long passion for locomotives, rail travel and art. In 2014 and 2015, Ellis turned his skilful hand back to travel posters, painting *Rotorua* and *Blue Baths*. The development of *Rotorua* features in documentary *Graphic Wonderland* (2014) directed by Peter Alsop and ibcfilms. Both posters are 100 x 60cm, acrylic on board and feature locomotives operated and permitted for use in the posters by Steam Incorporated, Paekakariki.

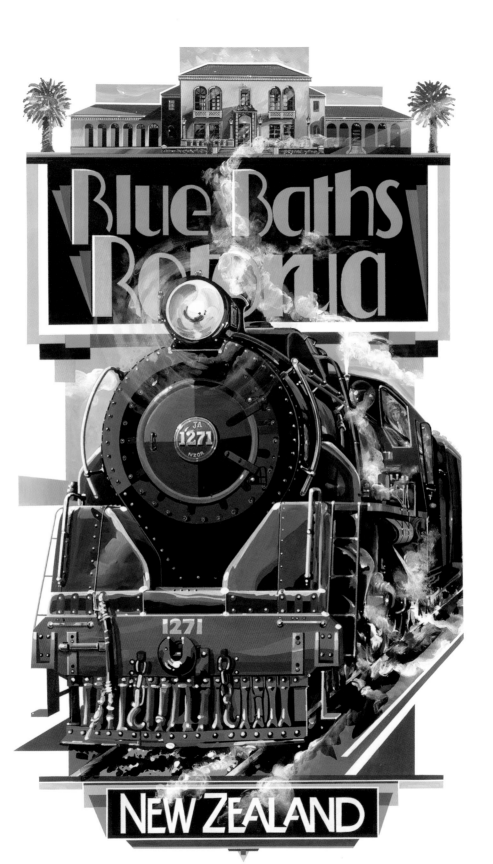

But it wasn't all plain sailing, particularly when it came to the arch enemy of rail, the car. By 1927, New Zealand was one of the most motorised countries in the world, a bleak outlook for rail unless the publicity drive could shift another gear. As it happened, a very driven Prime Minister and Railways Minister, Gordon Coates, had visited London for the 1926 Imperial Exhibition. Impressed with the progressive publicity methods of the world's best railways, he returned hell-bent on creating a new Publicity Branch. A further full-on publicity assault would occur.

In the case of the Railways, it's a surprising fact that the design division of a government agency would dominate outdoor advertising for about 70 years. Private design studios and advertising agencies played critical roles – Chandler & Co., Illots, Carlton Carruthers and Haythornthwaite to name a few – but it was the government studios that took centre stage. The Tourist Department's National Publicity Studios would really raise the travel poster bar, through artists like Leonard Mitchell (on external commission), Marcus King, George Bridgman, Howard Mallitte, Peter Read and Alan Collins.

CREATING IDENTITY

While motivated abroad, the publicity drive forged a new relationship for New Zealanders with their country. The countryside was open for business, offering rejuvenation from the ills of a modernising world – 'Thousands of feet above worry level' one Mt Cook slogan would read. The democratisation of travel, including campaigns to 'see your own country first', was so successful that churches would protest the Government's role in making nature a respectable weekend alternative. New Zealanders, themselves, would also patriotically send picturesque poster stamps (undenominated 'cinderellas') around the world as part of the publicity drive.

There were plenty of other events and locations that shaped New Zealand's identity. The first woman to summit Mt Cook, Australian Freda Du Faur in 1910, generated much attention and encouraged women to take to the great outdoors – something early

Right: The first Hermitage was built at Mount Cook in 1884, soon after the start of New Zealand's mountain tourism. This poster, largely relying on typography to do its job, likely dates from around 1930. Both the Tourist and Railways Departments worked hard to promote 'the alpine playground', including with other transport and accommodation providers given rail didn't reach Mount Cook and some other attractions. A number of progressive marketing initiatives were pursued. New Zealanders were also targeted, contrasting the refreshment and rejuvenation of a mountain visit to the smoke, fumes and ills of a modernising society.

Following pages: Alan Collins, former Art Director and Manager of the Tourist Department's National Publicity Studios, has referred to *Wild Flowers of New Zealand* (100 x 60cm) as a leading example of poster production. The poster was designed by Eugene Collett in 1966, but the success of the poster is owed equally to screen printer Gerald Phillips. The poster required 19 intricate stencils to be hand-cut by Phillips to create the layered colouring and depth of the image. The poster stands as a tribute to lithographers and screen printers – seldom recognised for their production work – who translated an original painting by the designing artist into a poster capable of mass production.

GO TO
MT. COOK
HERMITAGE
THIS WEEK END
£4.11.3
INCLUDING
ACCOMMODATION
Gov. RAILWAYS

Wild flowers of
NEW ZEALAND

PRICE ONE SHILLING

THE

WITNESS

CHRISTMAS

ANNUAL
1907

 IN THE LAND OF FINE SPORT
AND GOOD WOMEN.

PUBLISHERS: THE OTAGO DAILY TIMES AND WITNESS NEWSPAPER CO., LIMITED, DUNEDIN, N.Z.

publicity, surprisingly in wider social context, actively promoted. One artistic magazine cover trumpeted New Zealand as a 'land of fine sport and good women'. New Zealanders also liked being below ground as much as on top of it – Waitomo, the home of glow-worm caves, was the most successful of New Zealand resorts in the 1920s. Other key locations included Whanganui (for its famous Drop Scene); Lake Waikaremoana; Te Aroha and Helensville – none of these top the tourism pops today. Interestingly, Auckland – now home to over one quarter of New Zealand's population – was very seldom mentioned in early tourism material, and even less frequently presented in tourism art.

Buoyed by developments in the 1920s and 1930s, New Zealand would prepare for a very significant event – its first Centennial Exhibition, a big deal for the youngest country in the world. New Zealand's first Labour government was in power and, as part of a nation coming of age, it saw the chance for a comprehensive update of New Zealand's image – a celebration of what we'd achieved and a galvanising initiative for future success. With an expectation of drawing 4 million visitors, with world-class Art Deco buildings, the outbreak of the Second World War would unfortunately rain on the parade. Petrol was rationed and pleasure travel was off as ocean liners carried troops instead. In 1942, only 630 tourists would visit New Zealand. From a poster perspective, it was a shame that the masterpieces created – like Leonard Mitchell's official Centennial wahine (page 65) – weren't more widely enjoyed. But at least they were printed, as paper restrictions soon favoured wartime propaganda, a very different application of poster power.

A LASTING LEGACY

To give a sense of scale, in 1938 the Tourist Department distributed a massive 7 million brochures and 20,000 posters. By this time the Great Western Railway would note that 'the poster is a work of art, for the production of which world famous artists have been employed; ... commercial art has become a thing of beauty'.

Despite that proliferation and adoration, there has been a common misconception in New Zealand that early commercial art was for those unable to attain higher artistic dreams and, accordingly, not worth the art world's serious attention. In reality, commercial artists were at the forefront of developing a modern New Zealand art, while other artists looked back to conservative English painting roots. As Hamish Keith has put it: 'It is in the art of the poster that artists use their imagination and invention to unashamedly celebrate and reveal the uniqueness of the New Zealand scene.' Guy Somerset of the *Listener*

Left: From about 1900, the Christmas editions of leading magazines – such as *Free Lance*, the *Auckland Weekly News* and the *Otago Witness* – featured impressive colour covers that often touted New Zealand's tourism assets. This cover related to the 'Sportsman's Paradise', a promotional theme used extensively by the Tourist Department, with an intriguing statement about the complementarity of fine sport and good women. Source: *The Otago Witness*, Christmas Annual, 1907, ODT & Witness Newspapers Co, Image courtesy Hocken Library.

captured the tension in reviewing the full-length version of *Selling the Dream*: 'Imagine an alternative history of New Zealand art where the ground-breaking 20th Century painters we celebrated weren't Rita Angus, Toss Woollaston and Colin McCahon, but names such as Leonard Mitchell, Marcus King and Howard Mallitte. Never heard of them? That's because the works they produced were mainly for railway platforms and billboards here and overseas, not for the gallery wall.' What's more fascinating is that big names like Colin McCahon and Rita Angus were themselves heavily influenced by commercial art.

Notwithstanding the age of the images in this book, the intense impact and patriotic feeling remains very strong. But if you think a stripped-back poster style is easy, give it a try. And far from computer-aided design today, artists needed to create fonts, paint (and re-do) source paintings and hand-cut stencils or draw with greasy ink on lithographic stones. The arresting effectiveness of the images is a tribute to the skill of the artists. The fact that the images have lived on with contemporary appeal – in contrast to their disposable intent – is also testament to their significance to New Zealand's art and cultural history.

In spite of New Zealand's isolation from the rest of the world, its development has been entrepreneurial and impressive. It's even more remarkable how New Zealand, starting behind others as the world's youngest country, quickly generated some of the highest incomes and wellbeing benefits in the world. Tourism and travel posters were at the coalface of this success. Decades on, far from their archival worth, the posters still impress and remind us how lucky we are to live and play in New Zealand.

Right: When it comes to tourist attractions, several countries offer mountains, glaciers and thermal activity but only New Zealand can claim a unique Māori culture. Maoridom was a huge asset – New Zealand's exotica – and drawcard from the commencement of the Tourist Department's publicity drive. Whereas most posters of Māori women featured youthful 'Māori maidens', this poster is a rare portrait of a kuia, a female elder (see full poster on page 105). Her identity is unknown, but the poster itself dates from 1939 and can be seen on pages 86-87 at the Department's Centennial display. The poster was designed by George Bridgman, the Department's Art Director, and was an early example of a screen printed poster, something the Department proudly touted at the time as a printing breakthrough. Bridgman can also be seen painting the poster in the Department's 1939 'Behind the Scenes' film (featured in the documentary *Graphic Wonderland*). An important difference of this poster to others of Māori subjects is its cultural respect, with Bridgman profiling the greenstone hei-tiki as a precious and significant artefact, carefully nurtured by the kuia under an intent gaze. By contrast, New Zealanders still enjoy a 'tiki tour' today – a wandering exploration – despite the term trivialising hei-tiki. Images, for example, of Māori wearing ceremonial garb for daily duties were also culturally wrong. However, while many of the posters look out of place today, interpretation must keep in mind a social context some 60-90 years ago.

SCENIC WONDERLAND

The idea that New Zealand is a 'scenic wonderland' has its origins in ancient Europe and Africa. Imagining a perfect relationship between nature and humankind, the notion of paradise has been a common desire of the people of all continents and cultures throughout time. The word 'paradise' is derived from the French for the Garden of Eden, *Paradis*, and the Iranian word, *paradisus* for 'park'. So it is hardly surprising that colonisation and the immigration of Britain and Europe's population into the Pacific in the nineteenth century promised a new beginning in an idyllic land.

In New Zealand in the 1850s, surveyor artists like William Fox and Charles Heaphy promoted the benefits of voyaging halfway around the world, painting landscapes that revealed a paradise suitable for English settlement. In the twentieth century, the New Zealand Government Tourist Department also understood the value of such promises. From the scenic beauties of the country's national parks, to the fiords and mountains of Milford Sound and grandeur of Mt Cook, the Tourist Department promised a getaway to an experience with nature that – even today – still seems picture-perfect.

Leonard Mitchell

NEW ZEALAND FIORDS

Lithograph, 1930
Internal Affairs Department
1000 x 600mm

In its brightly coloured depiction of the forest and mountain,
Leonard Mitchell's view through the bush into Fiordland reveals
the modern style and design of the 1930s. Yet, as a professional
artist, Mitchell also had a knowledge of European art and the
influence of seventeenth-century landscape painting is evident in
this poster. The perfect world that Mitchell has created may be
based on a scene from the South Island, but its origins come from
Europe's art and culture.

Artist unknown

MT COOK FOR SUMMER

Lithograph, c.1935
Railways Department
875 x 565mm

Mt Cook's first Hermitage was built in 1884, but struggled to attract visitors due to the expense of the accommodation. In 1895, however, with the Government assuming ownership and improving facilities, it experienced a 'golden age' of mountain climbing. By the 1930s, Mt Cook was also part of an important tourist package that revealed the region as a 'playground'. Encouraged by affordable rail and road fares that included 'easy time-payment systems', visitors could amuse themselves in recreational activities, just like the youthful figure in this poster. She is surrounded by mountain daisies and has the evening comforts of the Hermitage to look forward to.

Charm of Mt. Cook

"THOUSANDS OF FEET ABOVE
WORRY LEVEL."

The splendour of the Southern Alps in the Mt. Cook region.

Height of Delight for your Holidays. The cosy Hermitage (a fully-licensed hotel) is famous as the Alpine social centre. Take Nature's tonic in the Alpine Wonderland thousands of feet above above worry level. Have the healthful happiness which lengthens life. See the greatest glaciers of the world's temperate zones. See the huge Hochstetter Ice-Fall. See the Marvellous Ice Caves which are like storied crystal palaces of fairyland. All manner of delightful side-trips amid enchanting scenes. Mount Cook, whose jewelled triple tiara gleams 12,349 ft. above the sea, one of the world's most majestic mountains, has a splendid retinue of noble peaks. Here, too, are stupendous glaciers far larger than the biggest "ice-rivers" of the Swiss Alps, and the way is easy to these huge courses of sparkling crystal. Everything in this bright realm of enchantment is on the gigantic scale ; everything pleases ; everything puts humanity on a high plane of exhilaration.

Full details from Offices and Agencies.

MT. COOK AND SOUTHERN LAKES TOURIST COY.

Following pages, left

Leonard Mitchell

MT EGMONT

Lithograph, 1934
Tourist Department
1000 x 600mm

As tourism grew in the late 1880s, Mt Cook and Mt Egmont were increasingly described as 'our glorious mountains'. By the 1930s, with the accompanying expansion of rail, scenic resorts and hotels, the country's natural landmarks acquired even greater appreciation as unspoilt landscapes that contrasted with busy city life. Mitchell's poster of Mt Egmont did more than urge local tourists to 'know your own country' – it also encouraged a sense of pride in New Zealand. It reminded people that, 'in no other country in the world is there concentrated such a wealth of scenic splendour'.

Following pages, right

Leonard Mitchell

MARLBOROUGH SOUNDS

Lithograph, 1934
Tourist Department
1000 x 654mm

Long before the inter-island ferry between the North and South islands was established, Marlborough was already a recognised tourist destination. Popular with pig and deer hunters in the first half of the twentieth century, by the 1930s it was increasingly favoured as a holiday destination for boating, fishing and swimming. Leonard Mitchell's poster of the Marlborough Sounds captures the region's attraction as an idyllic playground, with the artist taking a view through a clearing in the trees.

Left: From 1926 to 1940, the Railways Department published the monthly *Railways Magazine*. The magazine promoted the benefits of railways to New Zealand, and provided an ideal outlet for showcasing the Department's publicity work. The magazine was the brainchild of Gordon Coates, the Prime Minister and Minister of Railways, who had a very strong focus on progressive development of the Department's publicity effort. This advertisement for Mt Cook, 'thousands of feet above worry level', appeared in November 1937 (Vol. 12 No. 8).

MARLBOROUGH SOUNDS

GOVT
TOURIST
DEPT

NEW ZEALAND

Mt. Egmont, 8,260 ft.

NEW ZEALAND

Artist unknown

SEE THE GLORIES OF THE MILFORD TRACK

Screenprint, c.1935
Tourist Department
768 x 510mm

The Milford Track has been a major tourist attraction since the early 1890s. Discovered in 1888 by Quintin McKinnon and Ernest Mitchell, the route provided access from Lake Te Anau to Milford, and it was the earliest approach to Milford Sound. Involving a 53-kilometre hike through rainforests, wetlands and an alpine pass from Lake Te Anau to Milford, the region has been keenly protected over the past 100 years. This 1935 poster of the Milford Track promises the visitor the experience of a Garden of Eden.

SEE THE GLORIES OF THE

MILFORD TRACK

Book through the – NEW ZEALAND

GOVT TOURIST BUREAU TRAVEL SERVICE

Artist unknown

WAITOMO CAVES

Lithograph, c.1932
Railways Department
1005 x 635mm

While the Waitomo Caves were well-known to Māori, they gained national and international attention in the late 1880s, following Māori Chief Tane Tinorau and surveyor Fred Mace's discovery of the Glow-worm Grotto. In 1889 Tinorau, acting as a guide, opened the cave to visitors and numbers quickly soared. The Government acquired the land in 1904 and the Tourist Department managed the caves from 1905. This poster reveals the magic of the glow-worm caves in 1932 with lanterns and boats floating in the cavern for one of the 'Wonders of the world!'

Waitomo Caves

Glow Worm Grotto   *Wonder of the World!*

NEW ZEALAND

Full Information from

The High Commissioner for New Zealand - - - - 415 The Strand, LONDON, W.C. 2
New Zealand Trade and Tourist Commissioner - - - 320 Bay Street, TORONTO, CANADA
New Zealand Trade and Tourist Commissioner - - - - Martin Place, SYDNEY, AUSTRALIA
New Zealand Government Agent - - - - 59 William Street, MELBOURNE, AUSTRALIA
The General Manager, New Zealand Government Tourist Department - WELLINGTON, NEW ZEALAND

AND ALL TRAVEL AGENCIES

KNOW
Your Own Country

THIS country of ours is a land of which we can be justifiably proud, for in no other country in the world is there concentrated such a wealth of scenic splendour.

New Zealanders can see any of the following at very reasonable cost—

The unique underground caverns at Waitomo; the World's Wonder Walk to glorious Milford; Mt. Egmont; beautiful Queenstown in the Great Southern Lakes district; Lake Waikaremoana, " Sea of Rippling Waters "; the historic Marlborough Sounds or the Bay of Islands; Mt. Cook, thousands of feet above "worry" level; the Wanganui River; Chateau Tongariro, at National Park; Franz Josef and Fox Glaciers; the thermal wonders of Rotorua and Wairakei; Stewart Island; and Lake Taupo.

KNOW your own country! Let your nearest branch or agency of the Government Tourist Bureau assist you in planning your trip—it costs you nothing extra and saves you time and worry in the arrangement of train, boat and service car transportation, hotel accommodation, etc.

GOVERNMENT TOURIST BUREAU

Branches and Agencies in all Main Towns.

Linwood Lipanovic

BETTER FLY TO NEW ZEALAND

Screenprint, c.1960
TEAL
1000 x 600mm

Better Fly to New Zealand promotes the thermal
wonders of Rotorua. Lipanovic's knowledge of
modern art and design challenged both his clients
and audiences. Contrasting diagonal lines of text,
figures and form bring *Better Fly to New Zealand*
to life in a way that words could never achieve.
Lipanovic's poster makes it clear that Tasman
Empire Airways Limited (TEAL) is a modern
airline, promising its passengers to expect the
unexpected on their visit to New Zealand.

Linwood Lipanovic

BE THERE LONGER

Screenprint, c.1950
NAC
1000 x 600mm

In the early 1950s, the bold choice of a young
woman on water skis in *Be There Longer* by
Linwood Lipanovic, successfully positioned the
country's national airline, New Zealand National
Airways Corporation (NAC), as an exciting
way to travel. Lipanovic's poster anticipates the
popularity of a sport that had only just begun to
make its presence felt. Lipanovic was the son of a
Dalmatian migrant. He trained at the Elam School
of Fine Arts in Auckland and, following service in
the Second World War, worked for the advertising
agency, Carlton Carruthers, eventually becoming
a director of the company.

Left: The promotion of New Zealand's tourism assets was just as important domestically as the promotional efforts made abroad. New Zealanders
were encouraged to see their own country, increasing patronage of the growing rail network and further fuelling the Department's
advertising drive. Weekend travel became so popular, and a respectable alternative to weekend workshop, that churches complained to the
Government. This advert, making people think of attractions in completely different parts of the country, appeared in the *Railways Magazine*
in November 1936 (Vol. 10 No. 11).

BETTER FLY TO NEW ZEALAND
TEAL
TASMAN EMPIRE AIRWAYS LIMITED

be there longer

fly NAC

NEW ZEALAND NATIONAL AIRWAYS CORPORATION

Artist unknown

FAMOUS LAKES, MOUNTAINS, FIORDS

Lithograph, c.1930
Railways Department
1000 x 600mm

In the 1930s, the region of Otago established its reputation as a popular location for mountain climbing. Tourism grew – not only for climbers, but also for campers and sightseers and the region became known as a playground for winter and summer sports. *Famous Lakes, Mountains, Fiords* captures the spirit of an escape from the challenges of the working day, with campers immersed in a natural environment that also promises a good night's rest and the comforts of home.

Peter Read

CAREFREE HOLIDAYS

Screenprint, c.1955
Tourist Department
1000 x 600mm

Although hunting and fishing were popular activities from the early 1900s, for many New Zealanders the experience of being in the hills and bush was enough. A mix of socialising and exercise, from the 1940s to the 1970s, tramping clubs experienced significant growth. Peter Read's *Carefree Holidays* captures these elements. Read was employed by the National Publicity Studios in Wellington from 1939 but, in addition to the arts, he was also passionate about astronomy, gaining national attention throughout the 1960s as the front-person for popular television programmes, the *Night Sky* and *Horizon*.

Howard Mallitte

MILFORD SOUND

Screenprint, c.1955
Tourist Department
1013 x 636mm

Howard Mallitte's poster of Milford Sound tells us as much about modern art in New Zealand in the 1950s as it does about the region's natural beauties. The leisure boat with Mitre Peak as its colourful, stylish background suggests that Mallitte is interested in contemporary art. The strong, contrasting colours and design of this poster could have been taken from a modern European painting. Rather than appeal to the interests of earlier generations of tourists who wished to escape to the natural environment, Mallitte appeals to the tastes and comforts of urban New Zealanders in the late 1950s.

Milford Sound
NEW ZEALAND'S
FIORDLAND

FISHERMAN'S PARADISE

Mountainous and bush-covered New Zealand was well equipped for such active pursuits as climbing, hiking and skiing, however, nature had not provided it with fish suitable for the sport of angling. As a result, in the late 1860s, various fish from Britain and North America were introduced to this country's inland waterways and by 1904 it was being hailed as the 'Angler's (as well as Deerstalker's) Paradise', with brown and rainbow trout, salmon, perch and carp successfully acclimatised.

By comparison with its lakes and rivers, New Zealand's coastal waters have always been well-stocked and, therefore, ideal for big-game fishing. Māori traditionally caught swordfish and other species with handlines from canoes and Europeans first took to the sport in the early 1900s in the Bay of Islands. Local big-game fishing received a boost, thanks to popular American writer Zane Grey, who made four trips to New Zealand between 1926 and 1933. He established a base at Otehei Bay, on Urupukapuka Island in the Bay of Islands. This subsequently became a popular destination for deep-sea anglers from around the world during the summer, when large fish such as swordfish, marlin, tuna and shark were attracted to the warmer waters. Grey caught a record ten marlin in one day and a film of him landing a swordfish was made for screening overseas, while his books – including the bestselling 1926 *Tales of the Angler's Eldorado, New Zealand* – helped publicise the sport here.

Bill Haythornthwaite

FLY FISHING

Screenprint, c.1950
TEAL
900 x 600mm

This advertisement for Tasman Empire Airways Limited (TEAL) – the forerunner of Air New Zealand – exhorts people to come to New Zealand for its fishing. In this case the local sportsman is represented by a Māori tiki-like figure in a fly-fisherman's hat, who has successfully attracted the attention of a brown trout. The combination of individual elements in this poster reflects the prevailing style of the 1950s, while artist Bill Haythornthwaite made good use of the screenprinting process, ideal for creating large areas of flat colour. The leaping fish is effectively mirrored by its darker companion beneath the surface, while the hand-drawn lines and italic lettering add to the general playfulness of the composition.

FLY FISHING

FLY BY TEAL

to New Zealand

TASMAN EMPIRE AIRWAYS LIMITED → in association with QANTAS and B·O·A·C

Right

Howard Mallitte

BIG FIGHTING FISH

Screenprint, c.1955
Tourist Department
1000 x 600mm

This piece of big-game fishing action took place
in the Bay of Islands, identified by the distinctive
hole-in-the-rock of Piercy Island at top right. The
fact that this fish has not taken a line – as was
usually depicted in such promotional images –
suggests it is one that got away. The design takes
full advantage of the screenprinting process, with
its large areas of flat colour and simplified forms.
Also notable are the imaginative use of textures,
as seen on the 'big fighting fish' itself, and the
informality of the hand-done lettering. The foaming
surf and swirling green ocean add to the general
sense of immediacy and movement. In contrast,
the three men in the boat at top left appear
strangely becalmed.

Following pages

Artist unknown

RUSSELL

Lithograph, c.1923
Railways Department
752 x 1012mm

This poster depicts a successful day's fishing in the
Bay of Islands, a few years before Zane Grey's first
visit to the region. A sense of satisfaction is evident
as these sportsmen survey at least one large catch,
while circling seagulls suggest another is at hand.
This poster advises that local fishing grounds were
blessed with 'smooth water [and] giant fish'. This
was obviously a male preserve; according to Māori
lore, catching a swordfish single-handed was the
mark of a man. The red Art Deco typeface of
the period contrasts with the casual style of the
fisherman. The viewer's eye is drawn across the
strong diagonal created by their boat, towards
distant Russell and its perpetual summer.

RUSSELL BAY

By rail Wel
Here, amid

"When thou hast caught a swordfish singlehan

ISLANDS, NEW ZEALAND.
to Opua via Auckland, thence by boat 4 miles smooth water.
etual summer, the World's sportsmen battle with the giant fish
thou wilt be a Man, my Son".— Maori Proverb.

Harry Rountree

THE SPORTSMAN'S PARADISE

Lithograph, c.1930
Internal Affairs Department
920 x 660mm

This poster was produced during the period when the world's best known big-game fisherman, Zane Grey, was visiting New Zealand. Painted in a very fluid style, it captures the high drama as a fish takes the bait and leaps clear of the water. The artist has also caught the iridescent colours of the glistening fish, while the sense of movement is heightened by the bubbles and water trailing from its tail. The sportsman in the stern of the boat takes the strain on his rod, and the action has the attention of his three companions. The sea is dark and choppy, beneath a hot yellow sky. The tightly arcing form of the leaping fish captured here was also used on other promotions for New Zealand's big-game fishing.

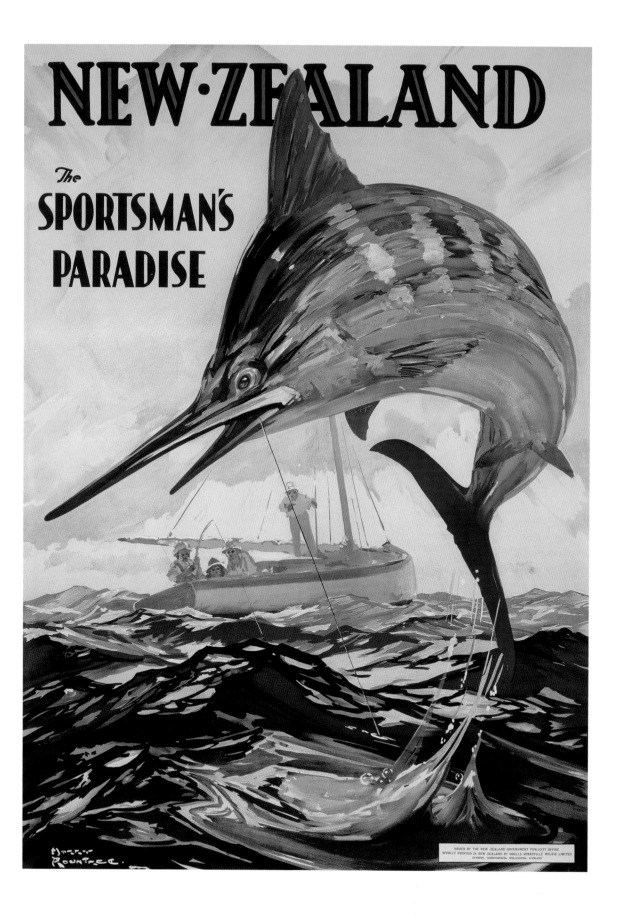

Maurice Poulton

FOR THE WORLDS BEST SPORT

Lithograph , 1936
Tourist Department
1000 x 600mm

This poster depicts a well-equipped and pipe-smoking angler casting his line in a typical New Zealand river. The image was ideal for reproduction by the lithographic process. The angler's arms and legs create opposing diagonals, adding to the sense of drama and concentrated effort, while his white shirt contrasts with the dark greens of the river and bush beyond.

FOR THE WORLDS BEST SPORT

NEW ZEALAND

LANDMARKS

A landmark is a natural or man-made feature that offers a guide for travelling, and also a word that represents our belief in significant events in history. The celebration of 100 years of Pākehā settlement in 1940 was considered a landmark occasion and was commemorated in regional and national celebrations. It reflected popular perceptions about the country's identity. The New Zealand Centennial Exhibition held in Wellington (November 1939–May 1940) was the most visibly successful centennial event. Held close to the airport at Rongotai, it was a carnival that featured a roller coaster and sideshows along with a trade fair that attracted 2.6 million visitors.

The Centennial acknowledged the country's material progress, as a partnership between hard work, new technology and improved transport systems all accommodated within the enduring natural beauty of the landscape. This was apparent in illustrations of farming and 'men alone' in high-country stations. Such popular images remained predominant in New Zealand culture for the next 40 years.

Leonard Mitchell

CENTENNIAL EXHIBITION

Lithograph, 1939
Tourist Department
1000 x 600mm

The 1940 centennial celebrations of the founding of New Zealand were five years in the planning and, from November 1939–May 1940, the exhibition in Wellington was its central attraction. Leonard Mitchell's poster for the Centennial shared much in common with popular cinema with its Art Deco buildings, showcasing a radiating light that had its origins in the German Expressionist film, *Metropolis* (1927). The wahine (woman) in this poster stands in for Pākehā aspirations. Posing as Zealandia, England's representative in the South Seas, she represents a youthful child who has come of age.

Right

Irvine Major

CANTERBURY CENTENNIAL

Screenprint, 1950
Publisher unknown
800 x 550mm

Although Wellington Mayor Thomas Hislop argued for a centralised centennial event in his city, the Under-Secretary of Internal Affairs, Joseph Heenan, maintained that celebrations should also be held in all towns and cities. The 1940 Centennial recalled historical milestones and looked to the future. With a generation of grandparents who had been settlers in the late nineteenth century still alive, the artist Irvine Major seemed aware that, for many New Zealanders, connections with the past were still tangible. Yet, the message in his poster is equally about progress, new and faster methods of communication, modern architecture and a determined nationalist spirit.

Following pages

Gerald Pryce

BRITISH EMPIRE EXHIBITION

Lithograph, 1924
The Empire Marketing Board
1270 x 1010mm

In the first half of the twentieth century, exhibitions and trade fairs played an important role in encouraging pride in one's country. Opening on 23 April 1924 in Wembley, London, the British Empire Exhibition attracted 25 million visitors. It encouraged trade between countries within the Empire and strengthen the idea that the British Empire remained strong after the First World War. Gerald Pryce's poster of the New Zealand landscape, its native flora, scenic beauty and – in the presence of farming stock – its economic assets, anticipated a popular image that would become dominant in New Zealand culture from the 1940s.

CANTERBURY
CENTENNIAL CELEBRATIONS
CHRISTCHURCH APRIL 8TH 14TH

LITHOGRAPH BY SPENCER PRYSE

BRITISH EMPIRE

SCENES OF EMPIRE
SERIES - - No P 33

APRIL

EXHIBITION 1924
OCTOBER

SCENES OF EMPIRE
SERIES - - No. P33

NEW ZEALAND
Celebrates

100 YEARS OF HISTORY

Following pages, left

Marcus King

SHEEP DRAFTING

Screenprint, c.1950
Tourist Department
765 x 510mm

Farming maintained an important role in defining New Zealand's identity from the mid-1940s to the 1970s. It offered reassurance about the quality of life. Marcus King's *Sheep Drafting* reveals both the beauty of nature and the productivity of the land and, by extension, its importance to the country's economy. This is a world that, by the 1960s, had become an imagined reality for many New Zealanders. A strong urban drift from the 1930s to the 1960s saw a million people migrate from the countryside to cities and towns.

Following pages, right

Marcus King

SOUTH WESTLAND

Screenprint, c.1955
Tourist Department
1000 x 600mm

The 1940 Centennial film, *One Hundred Crowded Years*, which documented the story of New Zealand's progress, was conceived with a storyline taken from Hollywood movies about the 'taming of the West'. Director R.W. Fenton chose a popular cowboy film, *Wells Fargo*, as the model for the pioneering period. Marcus King's *South Westland* is equally cinematic, locating the farmer against a panoramic landscape that could have been taken from any of a number of Westerns from the 1950s. It touches upon a relationship between humanity and the land that alludes to a history of settlement and the country's development for generations to come.

Left: New Zealand's Centennial celebrations saw the creation of come great commercial art. This brochure was published by Charles Haines Advertising, though the artist of the cover illustration is unknown. The cover speaks to a key theme of the event, New Zealand's coming of age; reflecting on a century of progress to look to the future with optimism.

SHEEP
DRAFTING

NEW ZEALAND

SOUTH WESTLAND
NEW ZEALAND

Marcus King

Artist unknown

ONE HUNDRED CROWDED YEARS

Screenprint, 1939
Tourist Department
1000 x 600mm

The commemorative film, *One Hundred Crowded Years*, had its origins in *A Nation is Built*, an Australian film that memorialised the 150th anniversary of New South Wales. *A Nation is Built* convinced Minister of Tourism, Hon Frank Langstone, that New Zealand's scenery would make an even more popular film. The film was divided into three parts: the pioneering generation, the country's development and New Zealand leading social reform. Its perspective of a country in which Māori and Pākehā were unified was an uplifting but misleading story of race relationships. The film led to the establishment of the National Film Studios in 1941.

MAORILAND

The concept of Maoriland as an alternative name for New Zealand first appeared in the 1860s. In the following years it proved particularly popular with poets and writers, the best known being Thomas Bracken, author of the national anthem and *Musings in Maoriland* (1890). 'Maoriland' was also chosen as the cable address for the Department of Tourist and Health Resorts, established in 1901.

Maoriland became an old-fashioned concept, but Māori continued to play a major part in this country's tourism industry. At the centre of this promotion lay Rotorua, home of the model Māori village at Whakarewarewa and extensive geothermal activity. Tourism images of Māori also moved with the times, from the romanticised views of the early 1900s to more realistic depictions by mid-century.

These posters reflect changing attitudes towards the depiction of Māori and the Māori world. The challenge for the designer was to produce an image that was both visually arresting and, according to the attitudes of the day, suitably respectful. When it comes to tourist attractions, several countries offer mountains, glaciers and thermal activity but only New Zealand can claim a unique Māori culture.

Bill Haythornthwaite and George Moore

FLY TEAL TO NEARBY NEW ZEALAND

Screenprint, 1952
TEAL
900 x 550mm

Tasman Empire Airways Limited (TEAL) was formed in 1940
and in the same year began a weekly flying-boat service
between Auckland and Sydney. A Wellington–Sydney flying-
boat service was inaugurated in 1950, and the following year
TEAL connected Christchurch and Melbourne by DC-4.
This screenprinted poster from 1952 encouraged Australians
to fly east, to 'nearby New Zealand', represented by blue skies,
mountain peaks, glaciers and geysers. The most prominent
attraction in this poster is the Māori carving in the foreground, a
stockade figure decorated in red ochre and further distinguished
by its moko (facial tattoo) and three-fingered hand.

Artist unknown

HAERE MAI

Chromolithograph, c.1935
Tourist Department
1015 x 632mm

The Whakarewarewa thermal region in Rotorua has been home to the Tūhourangi/Ngāti Wāhiao tribe for over 200 years. It has been a tourist attraction since the 1840s and was popularised by the visit of the 2nd Duke of Edinburgh in 1870–71. With the tourism industry in mind, a model village was built in 1909 before the establishment of a school for Māori carving in 1927. This poster shows residents of Whakarewarewa utilising the natural geothermal waters for their cooking. The woman with the child on her back, wrapped in her cloak, recalls *Ana Rupene and child*, a well-known and much-reproduced double portrait painted in 1878 by Gottfried Lindauer.

E.C. Waters

NEW ZEALAND VIA PANAMA CANAL

Lithograph, c.1930
Shaw Savill
1013 x 632mm

In the early 1900s the Whanganui River, the longest navigable river in the country, was known as the Rhine of New Zealand. A paddle steamer took tourists upriver to the famous Drop Scene, near Pipiriki, so named because the view looked like a painted theatrical landscape. This popular tourist spot has been used in this advertisement for shipping company Shaw Savill, with the ocean liner being represented by a Māori waka taua (war canoe). The canoe is distinguished by its elaborately carved tauihu (prow) and the ceremonial ihiihi, which consists of protruding poles covered with feathers. A chief stands near the prow, holding a taiaha (fighting staff) and brandishing a pounamu mere (greenstone club), while two crew members paddle furiously.

SHAW SAVILL LINE

NEW ZEALAND
VIA
PANAMA CANAL

Carl Laugesen

WONDERLAND OF THE PACIFIC

Chromolithograph, c.1935
Tourist Department
1005 x 640mm

This young Māori woman, enveloped in a kahu kiwi (kiwi feather cloak), featured in a wide range of tourism promotions in the mid-1930s. She was part of a tradition that began in the late nineteenth century with postcard images frequently showing young and attractive women. In the following decades such subjects became less ethnographic and conformed increasingly to European notions of glamour. This image of New Zealand concentrates on its natural and scenic attractions – mountain peaks and geysers and Māori culture, with the Chateau Tongariro located at the centre of the composition. Artist Carl Laugesen has managed to include his initials in the traditional tāniko (woven border) and has also drawn a parallel between the border and the geometric typeface of New Zealand.

VISIT NEW ZEALAND

· Wonderland of the Pacific ·

FULL INFORMATION FROM

The High Commissioner for New Zealand - - - - 415 The Strand, LONDON, W.C. 2
New Zealand Trade and Tourist Commissioner - - - 320 Bay Street, TORONTO, Canada
New Zealand Trade and Tourist Commissioner - - - Martin Place, SYDNEY, Australia
New Zealand Government Agent - - - - - 360 Collins St., MELBOURNE, Australia
The General Manager, New Zealand Government Tourist Department WELLINGTON, New Zealand
AND ALL TRAVEL AGENCIES

C. S. W. LTD.

Travel

SEPTEMBER, 1936

•

35 CENTS

IN THIS ISSUE

Following pages, left

Marcus King

ROTORUA

Screenprint, c.1950
Tourist Department
1000 x 600mm

The Pohutu Geyser (pōhutu meaning 'big splash'
or 'explosion') provides a dramatic background to
the Māori village of Whakarewarewa in Rotorua.
The main geyser in the area – Pohutu – performs
up to 20 times per day and can reach heights
of 30 metres. Also prominent in this image is a
small pātaka (store house), raised to protect its
contents from kiore (rats) and other predators.
Such structures could be up to six metres off the
ground, elevated on posts or tree trunks. In front
of the whare nui (meeting house) a trio of Māori
women are preparing flax fibre for weaving.

Following pages, right

Marcus King

MAORI CHIEF

Screenprint, c.1950
Tourist Department
1015 x 635mm

The appeal of the image of a Māori chief was long
recognised by early advertisers and achieved official
recognition when the second Māori King, Tawhiao,
was selected for inclusion on the New Zealand
£1 note from 1934 to 1940. A decade later Topia
Peehi Turoa, Chief of Ngati Patu-tokotoko was
used to promote the country's tourism industry.
Making imaginative use of a limited range of
colours, this screenprinted poster is an impressive
depiction of chiefly authority, marked by the
pair of huia feathers in the hair, full moko (facial
tattoo), pounamu (greenstone) ear pendants and
korowai (feather cloak) over the left shoulder.
The silhouettes of a meeting house, palisade and
carved figure in the background add to the sense of
mystery and mana (authority) commanded by this
face of New Zealand.

Left: In around 1935, Carl Laugesen designed one of the great Māori-themed posters of New Zealand's early tourism art. The inclusion of
diverse subject matter in the poster – wahine, a geyser, a mountain and a sophisticated resort – looks effortless and well-integrated; a mark
of an accomplished graphic designer. The image was so successful and alluring that it appeared on the cover of an American travel magazine
in September 1936; a rare and important example of international recognition of New Zealand's poster art. The magazine was published by
Robert M. McBride and Co.

ROTORUA

New Zealand

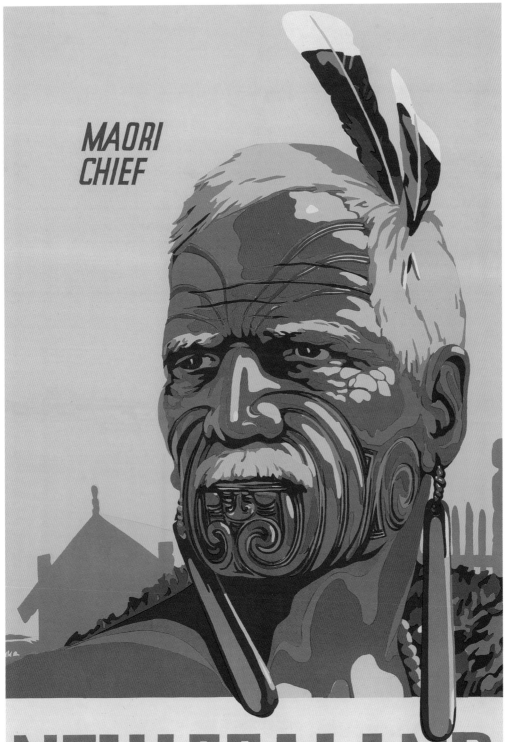

MAORI
CHIEF

NEW ZEALAND

Marcus King

SOUTH PACIFIC WONDERLAND

Screenprint, c.1955
Tourist Department
1010 x 600mm

During the 1950s, New Zealand enjoyed an increasing number
of visitors from overseas and received additional publicity when
the 1956 Melbourne Olympic Games drew the world's attention
to the South Pacific. In this poster from the mid-1950s, a pair of
(presumably) overseas guests admire one of the regular performances
of the Pohutu Geyser at the Whakarewarewa thermal village in
Rotorua. This poster acknowledges the changing attitudes towards
the depiction of Māori. By mid-century, the romanticism of earlier
decades was giving way to a more direct and contemporary view, and
the Māori guide seen here has combined European garments with her
feather cloak and piupiu (flax skirt).

NEW ZEALAND
South Pacific Wonderland

George Bridgman

NEW ZEALAND

Screenprint, 1935
Tourist Department
1000 x 600mm

At various times all sections of Māori society have been considered suitable subjects for tourism publicity, from babies on their mothers' backs to young maidens, warriors and the elderly. The latter category includes battle-scarred chiefs and kūia (elderly women) who were frequently portrayed in Europeanised dress and smoking pipes. In the early 1900s, well-known painter Charles F. Goldie recorded many such individuals. These nostalgic reflections captured the dignity of old age and the changing world of the Māori, and George Bridgman provided an updated and more upbeat interpretation for this poster in 1939.

NEW ZEALAND

REST AND RECREATION

New Zealand's diverse geography – from thermal activity to glaciers – has long been the basis for its tourism industry. With the more active tourist in mind, there was an early emphasis on hunting, fishing and bush walks and the increasing range of options led to this country being labelled the 'Scenic Playground of the Pacific'. Early promotional material was aimed at the international traveller but, by the 1930s, it had shifted to appealing to New Zealanders to get out and enjoy their own country. By now they could take advantage of an extensive rail network, coupled with connections by road and coastal steamer, and it was no coincidence that many of the more memorable tourism posters were produced by the Railways Studios.

Another of New Zealand's claimed attractions was the weather, and so posters attempted to lure holiday-makers to the sun, as at Tauranga or Timaru. One region that has long been at the centre of the national tourism industry is the 'Hot Lakes District', based on Rotorua. Once the gateway to the 'Eighth Wonder of the World', the Pink and White Terraces (destroyed in the 1886 eruption of Mt Tarawera), it continues to attract visitors with its thermal activity and displays of Māori life and culture.

Artist unknown

TIMARU BY THE SEA

Lithograph, 1936
Railways Department
880 x 570mm

A beach belle in a fashionable swimming costume leaps across the
golden sand, embracing the Timaru sunshine. This is a remarkably
bold image, with a single figure dominating the composition. It also
makes masterful use of large areas of flat colour, while a number of
beach-goers are effectively reduced to simple sun-bronzed shapes.
The four-word message says it all, while the wavy line through
'Timaru' reinforces the connections with the sea. This image shows
the beach at Caroline Bay, while its other facilities – including
grassed areas and a soundshell for open-air entertainment – can be
seen beneath the young lady's left arm. The poster was produced at a
time when the beach had become a popular place for swimming and
sunbathing. A similar image had been used on a poster promoting
the Napier Carnival in 1933.

Artist unknown

GET IN THE 'QUEUE' FOR QUEENSTOWN

Lithograph, 1930
Railways Department
1000 x 600mm

Visitors join the 'Q' to enjoy a spectacular bird's-eye view of
Queenstown, on the shores of Lake Wakatipu, and the Remarkables
beyond. From here the holiday-maker could enjoy hunting, fishing,
tramping and skiing, justifying the claim that New Zealand was the
'Playground of the Pacific'. This poster makes playful use of type, as
seen in the modifications to the two 'a's of 'Zealand'. According to
the small type at the bottom, overseas visitors wishing to experience
this view for themselves were advised to 'queue' at tourist offices in
London, Toronto, Sydney and Melbourne.

Artist unknown

FOR HEALTHFUL HOLIDAYS

Lithograph, 1932
Railways Department
890 x 575mm

Several tourist spots in the 1930s appealed to the health-conscious
holiday-maker, offering the benefits of hot mineral springs.
The existence of such a natural resource at Hanmer, in North
Canterbury, was known by the late 1850s, and a settlement was later
developed by the Department of Tourist and Health Resorts. The
poster shows the Spanish-style lodge, completed in 1932, with its
exotic colonnades, arches and bell tower, which gave accommodation
here an international reputation. In addition to the therapeutic
benefits of the mineral waters, guests could also enjoy a game of
tennis or a round of golf.

Following pages: The Railways Department periodically used its poster designs as part of advertisements in the *Railways Magazine. Come South!*, celebrating some of Christchurch's heritage architecture, appeared in October 1935 (Vol. 10 No. 7), while *Healthful Hanmer*, an example of a strong focus on health resorts at the time, ran in February 1933 (Vol. 7 No. 8).

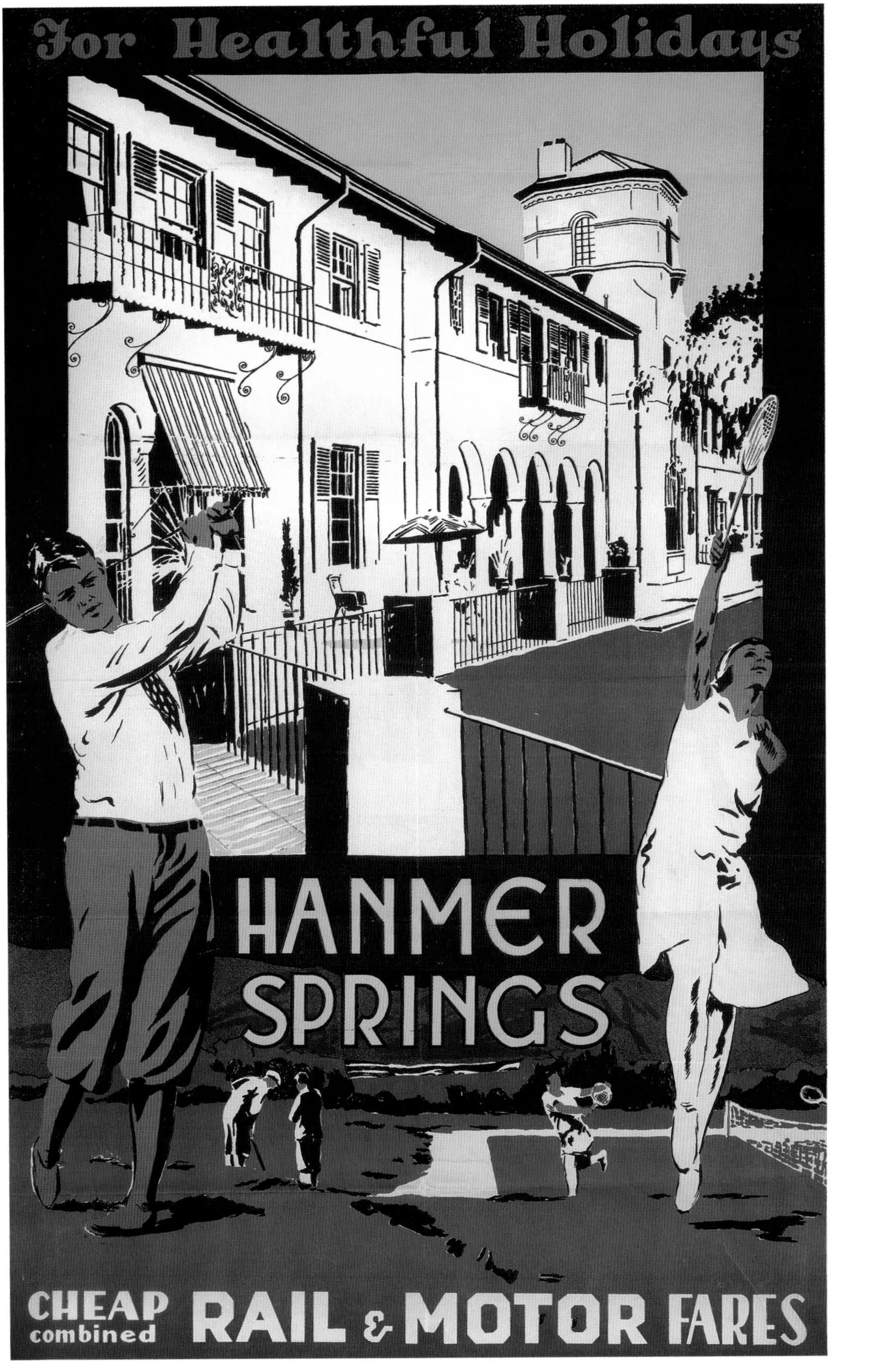
For Healthful Holidays
HANMER SPRINGS
CHEAP combined RAIL & MOTOR FARES

HEALTHFUL HANMER

Try The Lodge, Hanmer, for a health-giving South Island holiday.

Excellent cuisine —willing service.

The way to happiness:

HEALTHFUL HOT SPRINGS TONIC CLIMATE.

Book through by rail from anywhere in New Zealand, making connection with Mockett's Motors to Hanmer.

SPA OF THE SOUTH ISLAND

Artist unknown

CHRISTCHURCH

Lithograph, 1935
Railways Department
1010 x 585mm

The Garden City of Christchurch, the doorway to the scenic wonders of the South Island, is represented by a shady corner of the River Avon. Beyond is Christchurch Cathedral, with smaller views of other accessible attractions – the mountains, lakes and hot springs – at the bottom of the composition. The emphasis here is on architectural features of Christchurch, once the most English of New Zealand cities. The design of this poster is in strong contrast to the more dynamic approach taken by others in the promotion of tourist spots around the country at this time. Even the typeface here is a conservative approach, evoking an illuminated medieval manuscript rather than the spirit of the 1930s.

NEW ZEALAND
SOUTH ISLAND
THE PLAYGROUND OF THE PACIFIC

CHRISTCHURCH

Sunny Lakes

Mountains and Glaciers

Hot Springs

with the Wonders "on the doorstep"!

RAILWAYS STUDIOS

Artist unknown

TAURANGA FOR WINTER SUNSHINE

Lithograph, 1934
Railways Department
900 x 550mm

This unusual image suggests a line from Coleridge's *Rime of the Ancient Mariner*: 'All in a hot and copper sky'. A cheery sun-bleached individual, casting a long black shadow, extends his hand and invites another into his solar orbit. The sun is evidently white-hot over the Bay of Plenty holiday spot of Tauranga, seen here sweltering in the warmest colours of the spectrum, red and orange. The slopes of the region's dominant geographic feature, Mt Maunganui, also receive the full benefit of golden sunshine.

Eugene Collett

NORTHLAND

Screenprint, c.1960
Tourist Department
765 x 508mm

This is a composite and rather conventional design, perhaps reflecting the difficulty of selecting one single attraction to represent the Far North of New Zealand. A leaping swordfish, however, does have some prominence at top left, promoting big-game fishing in the Bay of Islands. Also shown are a sandy beach, a citrus orchard and one of the world's great trees, the mighty kauri, standing alongside another distinctive feature of the New Zealand bush, the nīkau palm. All the snapshots seen here are drenched in sunshine, reinforcing the 'sub-tropical' message and the region's reputation as the 'Winterless North'.

SUNNY SUB-TROPICAL

Northland

NEW ZEALAND

Howard Mallitte

WELLINGTON

Screenprint, c.1950
Tourist Department
765 x 510mm

This atmospheric view of Wellington has been
achieved with a restrained palette. It captures
the mood at the end of the day when the sun
disappears over the hills and the lights go on in the
city below. The only concession to strong colour
is the pillar-box red funnel on the ocean liner in
the harbour, then the latest word in international
travel. This composition, of areas of flat colour
and simplified forms – as in the hills, buildings
and number of twinkling lights – was ideal for the
screenprinting process and effectively conveys
the sense of the city by night.

Wall Cousins

WELLINGTON HARBOUR

Lithograph, c.1925
New Zealand Shipping Co Ltd
1016 x 1267mm

This large panorama of Wellington Harbour, as seen
from the hills above, was produced shortly after
the city's population had reached 100,000. The
artist has framed the view with native vegetation,
and also made effective use of strong colours,
in particular the red border and foreground, and
the deep blue that cuts across the centre of
the composition. There is a slight breeze on the
harbour, and some of the vessels seen here may
belong to the New Zealand Shipping Company,
which commissioned the poster. It seems safe
to assume that this image, of a harbour city
surrounded by green hills and expansive areas
of open countryside, was designed to appeal to
overseas visitors.

New Zealand Life and Scenes - Number Seven -
CITIES OF NEW ZEALAND
WELLINGTON

Leonard Mitchell

BLUE BATHS

Lithograph, 1935
Tourist Department
1000 x 660mm

This poster was produced in 1935, only a year or so after Rotorua's Blue Baths were opened. It was designed by one of New Zealand's most successful graphic designers, Leonard Mitchell, who has, unusually, given this image a bold black border. The focus of the Blue Baths (so named because of the colour of the mineral water) was on recreation, in contrast to the curative properties claimed of other bath houses in Rotorua. The Blue Baths also offered mixed-gender bathing for the first time in New Zealand, reflecting the more relaxed attitudes of the post-First World War period. The emphasis in this poster, however, is on the two female figures in the foreground, whose attention is on the pool.

BLUE BATHS, ROTORUA

GOV?
TOURIST
DEPT

NEW ZEALAND

Right

Artist unknown

ROTORUA: NATURE'S CURE

Lithograph, 1932
Railways Department
1010 x 633mm

This poster was aimed at the holiday-maker wishing to enjoy heath-giving recreation, with the top panel illustrating some of 'Nature's Cures' in action. Here the unique combination of 'magic mud' and modern electrical devices was, allegedly, able to cure rheumatism, gout, sciatica, lumbago and other such troubles. Even those who were not ill, but rather jaded or run-down, were advised to refresh mind and body in Rotorua, which was also promoted as 'Cureland'. This poster appealed to overseas visitors. In addition, visitors could relax playing croquet, tennis or golf or enjoy the angling and the scenery.

Following pages

Marcus King

CHATEAU TONGARIRO

Screenprint, c.1935
Tourist Department
635 x 1010mm

In 1929 the Chateau Tongariro hotel and resort complex opened at the central North Island settlement previously known as Whakapapa. It became the centre for sightseeing and winter sports in the region. The neo-Georgian style Chateau was built by a private company and was renovated in the late 1940s before, in 1957, being taken over by the Government Hotel Tourist Corporation of New Zealand. This image, by graphic artist and landscape painter Marcus King, is distinguished by its border-free horizontal (landscape) format. The various elements – skiers, and golfers in front of the Chateau and Mt Ruapehu – have been reduced to simplified forms, ideal for production by the screen-printing process.

Rotorua

AIX MASSAGE DOUGHE

SCHNEE MULTIPOLAR ELECTRIC BATH

HIGH FREQUENCY VALVE

Thermal Waters

Health and Recreation

Nature's Cure

FULL INFORMATION FROM—

The High Commissioner for New Zealand	415 The Strand, LONDON, W.C. 2
New Zealand Trade and Tourist Commissioner	320 Bay Street, TORONTO, Canada
New Zealand Trade and Tourist Commissioner	Martin Place, SYDNEY, Australia
New Zealand Government Agent	59 William St., MELBOURNE, Australia
The General Manager, New Zealand Government Tourist Department	WELLINGTON, New Zealand

AND ALL TRAVEL AGENCIES

NEW ZEALAND

ENJOY a
PERFECT
HOLIDAY
at the

CHATEAU T
NATION

ONGARIRO
L PARK

TRAINS AND PLANES

The close relationship between comfortable and affordable travel and tourism were evident as early as the 1860s with the opening of the Otira Gorge Road between Canterbury and the West Coast. It meant that, by the late 1870s, Otira's spectacular landscape was a popular subject for artists. (It had been singled out as a highlight at the New Zealand and South Seas Exhibition in Dunedin in 1889). Throughout the twentieth century, changes in tourists' expectations about the best way to travel, whether by train, plane or car, were all promoted with a promise of escape, excitement and comfort. Expanding rail networks in the late nineteenth century were popular until the 1960s, when they were challenged by the family car and time-saving options of flight in the 1970s. Although New Zealand Railways sought to compete, introducing the Silver Star – a fashionable night train that promised greater comfort on the North Island main trunk route – nothing could halt the inevitable competition of NAC's Boeing-737 jets.

Artist unknown

AIR-CONOMY TOURS

Screenprint, c.1955
TEAL
1000 x 600mm

Commercial flights linking New Zealand and Australia began in April 1940, with Tasman Empire Airways Limited (TEAL) launching its first trans-Tasman services from Auckland to Sydney. The idea for a trans-Tasman airline was first proposed in 1918 by Sir Frederick Sykes, Controller-General of Civil Aviation in Great Britain, who wished to bring the British Empire's colonies closer together. By the 1950s, TEAL had extended its services from the Pacific to Asia and Europe, developing an international network that anticipated the jet era of the 1960s, and the promise of excitement and romance expressed in popular movies such as *Come Fly with Me* (1963).

AIR-CONOMY TOURS
of NEW ZEALAND
TEAL
MORGAN
New Zealand's International Airline

Artist unknown

FOR YOUR HOLIDAYS

Lithograph, 1948
Railways Department
886 x 568mm

As early as the 1890s, New Zealand Railways equally promoted their freight services as well as the advantages for the local tourist. They offered special deals for travellers during the Christmas, Easter and school holidays. From the 1920s they promoted travel by rail in New Zealand to local and international tourists. With increasing leisure time, New Zealanders could afford longer holidays, particularly over the Christmas and New Year period. In addition, the declining size of families meant cheaper and more manageable holidays. As cars were still a luxury for many, New Zealand Railways reaped the financial benefits during this boom period throughout the 1920s and 1930s.

Following pages, left

Kate Olsen

WHEN TIME MEANS MONEY

Photo-mechanical print, 1936
Union Airways
886 x 570mm

When Time Means Money represents a bold statement by Union Airways, a new domestic airline established in 1934. Bringing together the economic interests of the Union Steam Ship Company and Cook Strait Airways, the companies amalgamated, flying between Palmerston North and Dunedin with stops in Blenheim and Christchurch. Two years earlier, New Zealander Jean Batten had fuelled the popularity of flight and captured the imagination of the entire country by flying solo from England to Australia. This created an excitement that helped Union Airways' marketing campaign.

Following pages, right

Kate Olsen

SPEED COMFORT REGULARITY

Photo-mechanical print, 1936
Union Airways
886 x 570mm

Appropriately named *Karoro*, or gull, the de Havilland 86 Express in this Art Deco poster for Union Airways, offers a cutaway view inside the plane, providing the reassurance of spaciousness and comfort for passengers and their luggage. The de Havilland Express was a four-engine passenger aircraft designed in the 1930s and manufactured by the de Havilland Aircraft Company. As a woman working in commercial art in the 1930s, Kate Olsen was in good company. New Zealand's art schools had trained artists in the traditions of the Arts & Craft Movement, skilful in observational drawing and design. Also employed as commercial artists in the 1930s were Rita Angus, her sister Jean, Avis Higgs and Joan Edgar.

Left: See New Zealand by Train and Railway Road Services is an impressive line drawing that appeared in the *Railways Magazine* in April 1940 (Vol. 15 No. 1). Whereas some Tourist Department artists were permitted to sign their work – such as Marcus King, Leonard Mitchell and George Bridgman – artists at the Railways Studios weren't and, instead, the insignia 'Railways Studios' was consistently used.

SPEED
COMFORT
REGULARITY

by Air

PALMERSTON N. - BLENHEIM - CHRISTCHURCH

UNION
AIRWAYS

Artist unknown

GOVERNMENT TOURIST DEPARTMENT

Screenprint, c.1955
Tourist Department
1000 x 600mm

By the 1950s, an established network of tourist facilities at major resorts and a comprehensive service of accommodation and transport saw a shift by the New Zealand Government Tourist Department from local to international tourism. This campaign focused on the promotion of this country's 'scenic wonders' and encouraged the New Zealand Government Travel Service to offer the international visitor an inclusive easy-to-book package. The imagery and style of this Art Deco poster from the Tourist Department in the mid-1950s reveal this new marketing, with an elegant and stylish promise of travel to a far-away place across the Pacific.

Agents for

NEW ZEALAND
GOVERNMENT
TOURIST
DEPARTMENT

Bookings for

RAIL · STEAMER · MOTOR · AIR
SERVICES & HOTEL ACCOMMODATION

Linwood Lipanovic

BE THERE LONGER

Screenprint, 1953
NAC
760 x 505mm

Be There Longer was singled out by design historian
Douglas Lloyd-Jenkins in *Forty Legends of New Zealand
Design* as the 'masterpiece' of Linwood Lipanovic.
The success of the poster resides in his response to
National Airways Corporation's (NAC) marketing
agenda for international flight in the 1950s. How was
flying different from sailing, driving or rail? In three
words and an unforgettable image of a figure, relaxing
on the beach (positioned to reflect the shape of the
silhouetted plane above), Lipanovic puts forward an
unchallengeable response. Swiftness of flight will reward
the traveller with more time to relax and take in the
beauty and pleasures of New Zealand.

Arthur Thompson

YOUR NEW ZEALAND HOLIDAY

Screenprint, c.1960
TEAL
970 x 630mm

Throughout the 1950s and 1960s, international flight represented a widespread confidence in Western society – exotic and far-away places were waiting to be experienced. *Your New Zealand Holiday*, by Auckland artist Arthur Thompson, is decidedly modern with its abstract and decorative depiction of a cabbage tree. The animated exclamation of the hei tiki as TEAL flies through its open-gaped mouth however, is more problematic. Representing evidence of 'cultural imperialism', the looney-tunes depiction of a memorial to ancestors, also reveals a long-standing cultural divide between Māori and Pākehā in the post-war era.

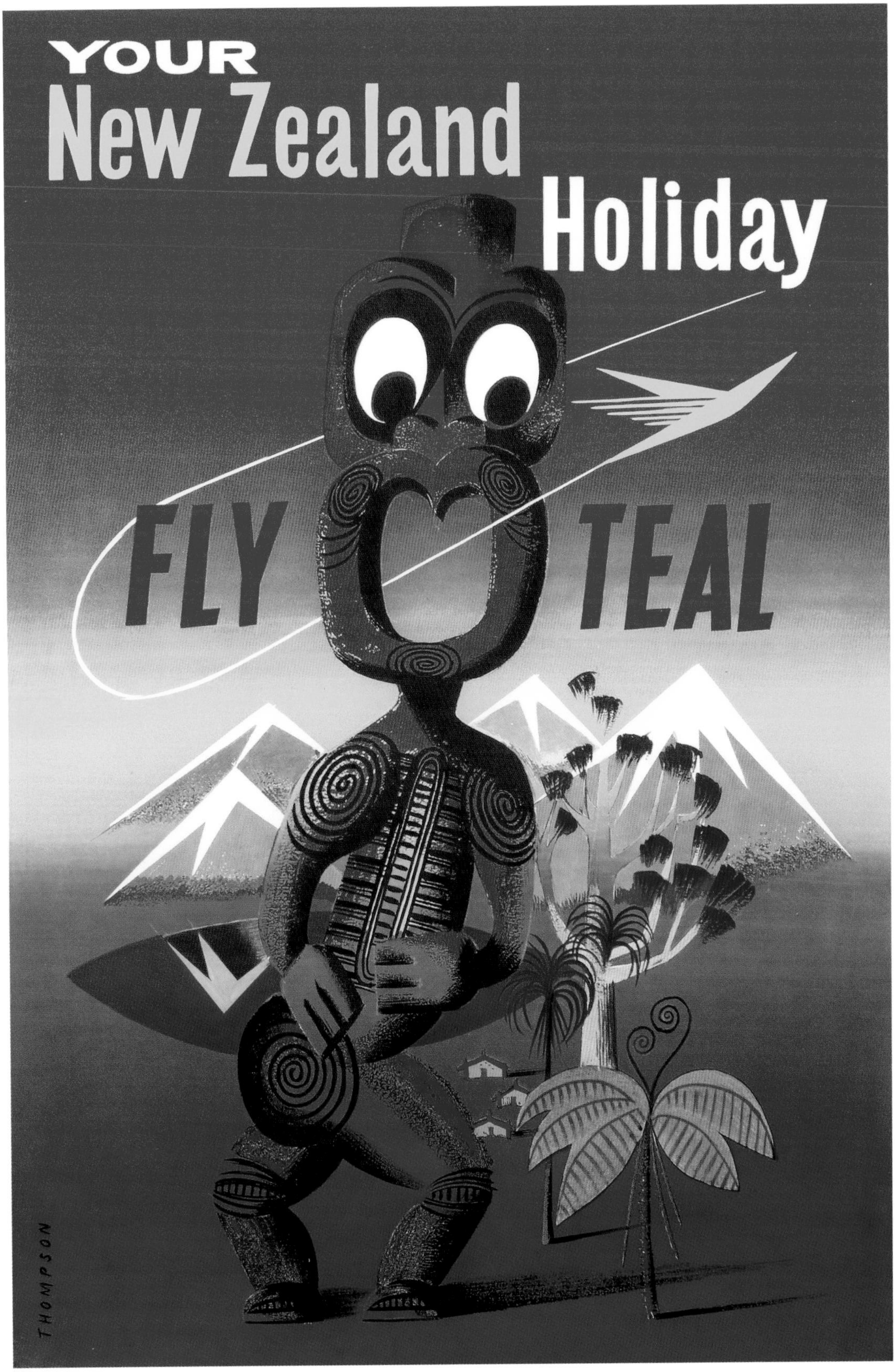
YOUR
New Zealand
Holiday
FLY TEAL
THOMPSON

Dennis Beytagh

NEW ZEALAND

Lithograph, 1960
Tourist Department
1012 x 630mm

While the Tourist Department shifted its attention to international tourism in the 1950s, its marketing strategies remained similar to those from the 1880s, promising an experience of the world's best beauty spots. Writing on the Wakatipu Lake District in 1888, Alfred H. Duncan claimed: '... the beauties of the Swiss Lakes, the grandeur of the Rocky Mountains, and the glacier-clothed peaks of the Himalaya mountains are as nothing when compared with the deep blue waters of the Wakatipu ... and the glacier-covered Earnslaw'. Dennis Beytagh's *New Zealand* also promises a diversity of outdoor experiences: fishing, skiing, volcanoes, yachting, mountain climbing, hunting and indigenous culture.

NEW ZEALAND

SHAW
The FLAG
that circles
the WORLD_
VIA Panama Canal
and
VIA Australia

ACKNOWLEGEMENTS

This publication and related exhibition would not have been possible without the generous support of all the organisations and individuals (including those who gave image permissions) who enabled *Selling the Dream: The Art of Early New Zealand Tourism*, by Peter Alsop, Dave Bamford and Gary Stewart to be published in 2012.

Appreciation is also recorded to the following people and organisations for their role in the development and staging of the *Selling the Dream* exhibition:

- Anthony Wright and the staff of Canterbury Museum;

- Warren Feeney and Richard Wolfe for co-curating the exhibition;

- Private collectors who loaned their works to make the exhibition possible, including Alan Craig, Peter Haythornthwaite and Terri Lipanovic;

- Tourism New Zealand and KiwiRail for their support for the *Selling the Dream* project and permissions to use relevant images (along with other institutions and organisations that have similarly supported the resurfacing and sympathetic celebration of this historic material);

- Karl Chitham for initial development work on the exhibition;

- Alan Collins, Barry Ellis, Dick Frizzell, Hamish Keith, Barbara Lyon, Margaret Morris and Gerald Phillips for interview footage used in the exhibition;

- Phil Boltt for the production of the interview film 'vignettes';

- ibcfilms for co-directing (with Peter Alsop) and producing the documentary *Graphic Wonderland* (http://vimeo.com/114574856);

- John Collie of Christchurch Art Gallery, Te Puna o Waiwhetu, for exhibition photography (including some of the close-up images used in this book); and

- Ronald Mottram Picture Framers for framing of the exhibition works.

Right: Marcus King's *South Pacific Wonderland* (see page 103 for full poster) features, Guide Rangi, a well-known Māori guide at Rotorua's Whakarewarewa Village, with tourists admiring the Pohutu Geyser. The poster was based on a photo taken by the National Publicity Studios, right down to the detail of Rangi's European scarf and footwear. King was the Tourist Department's premier poster artist from around 1940 until his retirement in 1961. He was also a skilled painter, excelling at Impressionism early in his career (mid-1920s) before also becoming the Department's go-to artist for large-scale landscape and documentary murals.

L.E. MITCHELL.

REMAINING IMAGE CREDITS

Page 1 – New Zealand Railways advertisement (text removed from box), *New Zealand Freelance Annual*, 2 December 1929.

Pages 6–7 (after Contents) – Government Tourist Bureau, Rotorua, Unknown, c.1937, Tourist Department, Alexander Turnbull Library 1/1-012014-F.

Page 8 (Foreword) – *Winter Sports at Tongariro National Park*, c.1960, Screen print, 77x51cm, Private collection (Available at Alexander Turnbull Library, Eph-D-TOURISM-1960-01).

Pages 10–11 (after Foreword) – Installation photo of Selling the Dream exhibition, Canterbury Museum, 2015. Photo by John Collie, Christchurch Art Gallery, Te Puna o Waiwhetu.

Pages 30–31 (before Scenic Wonderland) – Eric de Lacy (L) and Gerald Phillips, National Publicity Studio, B. Clark, 1957, Tourist Department, Archives New Zealand, AAQT 6401/26 A51164.

Pages 56–57 (before Fisherman's Paradise) – Railways Department window display, c.1935, Railways Album 11, Alexander Turnbull Library, PA1-f-060.

Pages 70–71 (before Landmarks) – L.C. (Leonard) Mitchell in his studio, Unknown, 1970, *Evening Post*, Alexander Turnbull Library EP-NZ Obits-MB to MI-01.

Pages 86–87 (before Maoriland) – Display stand of the Tourist and Publicity Department at the 1939/40 Centennial Exhibition, Alexander Turnbull Library, PA1-O-021-48.

Pages 106–107 (before Rest and Recreation) – George Moore, Haythornthwaite Studios, 1949, Whites Aviation, Alexander Turnbull Library, WA-20398-F.

Pages 134–135 (before Trains and Planes) – Paremata Station, Unknown, c.1955, Archives New Zealand, AAVK-W3493-B6869.

Pages 154–155 (before Acknowledgements) – Shaw Savill Lines, advertising hoarding, Album of Chandler & Co Ltd, 'Dominion Poster Service'. Image courtesy John Perry.

Every attempt has been made to obtain permission from the copyright owners to use these photographs and other imagery in the book; if any errors or omissions have occurred, please contact the publisher.

Left and back cover: The Art Deco Movement was pivotal in the development of poster art and a very contagious trend in New Zealand. The Art Deco style, characterised by stripped back images to essential colours and forms, was mastered by Leonard C. Mitchell, by far the most prodigious producer of tourism art in New Zealand from around 1925 to 1940. Curiously, Mitchell never worked for the Tourist or Railways Departments; instead being commissioned as the lead artist at Filmcraft, a private company whose primary business was creating tourism movies for the Government. Mitchell's pipe-smoking mountaineer (left) portrays a risky adventure as a serene experience; an image that Jim and Mary Barr recall greatly impressed Professor Charles Eldredge, a leading American art historian. In *Blue Baths* (1935) on the back cover, Mitchell frames the image with columns and foreground figures that naturally lead the viewer deeper into the image, an ancient technique called repoussoir (see full poster on page 129). In colour, form, composition and impact, the poster stands as a leading example of early graphic design in New Zealand.